Egyptian Treasures

Catherine Chambers

Crabtree Publishing Company
www.crabtreebooks.com

Author: Catherine Chambers
Editor: Crystal Sikkens
Project coordinator: Kathy Middleton
Production coordinator: Ken Wright
Prepress technician: Margaret Amy Salter
Series consultant: Gill Matthews

Every effort has been made to trace copyright holders and to obtain their permission for use of copyright material. The authors and publishers would be pleased to rectify any error or omission in future editions. All the Internet addresses given in this book were correct at the time of going to press. The author and publishers regret any inconvenience caused if addresses have changed or sites have ceased to exist, but can accept no responsibility for any such changes.

Picture credits:
Alamy Images: The London Art Archive 11b
Corbis: Burstein Collection 9b, Werner Forman 17, 18, Free Agents Limited 19, David Lees 10, Gianni Dagli Orti/The Picture Desk Limited 9t, Roger Wood 14
Dreamstime: David Campbell 4, Katy Odell 8br, Asier Villafranca 21
Fotolia: Freesurf 15t, Travis Hiner 20, Horticulture 13, Stanislav 12
Shutterstock: (Cover), Adam36 8bl, Robert J. Beyers II 8t, Mario Bruno 6, 16, Stephen Coburn 5b, Dainis Derics 7, Fatih Kocyildir 11t, Ulrich Willmünder 5t

Library and Archives Canada Cataloguing in Publication

Chambers, Catherine, 1954-
    Egyptian treasures / Catherine Chambers.

(Crabtree connections)
Includes index.
ISBN 978-0-7787-9946-7 (bound).--ISBN 978-0-7787-9968-9 (pbk.)

    1. Egypt--Antiquities--Juvenile literature.
2. Egypt--Civilization--To 332 B.C.--Juvenile literature.
I. Title. II. Series: Crabtree connections.

DT61.C465 2010   j932   C2010-901518-5

Library of Congress Cataloging-in-Publication Data

Chambers, Catherine, 1954-
  Egyptian treasures / Catherine Chambers.
    p. cm. -- (Crabtree connections)
  Includes index.
  ISBN 978-0-7787-9968-9 (pbk. : alk. paper) -- ISBN 978-0-7787-9946-7 (reinforced library binding : alk. paper)
  1. Egypt--Civilization--To 332 B.C.--Juvenile literature. 2. Egypt--Antiquities--Juvenile literature. I. Title. II. Series.

DT61.C426 2011
932--dc22

                                        2010008065

Crabtree Publishing Company
www.crabtreebooks.com   1-800-387-7650

Printed in the U.S.A./062010/WO20100815

Published in Canada
Crabtree Publishing
616 Welland Ave.
St. Catharines, Ontario
L2M 5V6

Published in the United States
Crabtree Publishing
PMB 59051
350 Fifth Avenue, 59th Floor
New York, New York 10118

CONTENTS

WHAT IS TREASURE?

Ancient Egypt's treasures help us look deep into the past. Each treasure is part of a puzzle that builds a picture of people's lives. Most treasures are **artifacts**, which are objects that craftspeople have made from many different materials. There would be no artifacts without one huge feature—the Nile River.

Traders used the Nile to carry their goods to faraway places.

The treasure of the Nile

Ancient Egypt grew up around its greatest treasure—the Nile River. People settled along its wide banks over 7,000 years ago. They came with herds of animals because the vast grasslands of North Africa had turned into a desert.

Fertile land

Every year **floodwater** from the Nile covered the land with rich, fertile soil. This soil was great for growing crops. Some people sold extra crops they didn't need for themselves. This meant they grew wealthy and became powerful rulers.

Some artifacts are made of gold and precious jewels—others simply of wood or stone.

Precious pyramids

Egypt's kings and queens employed people to make useful and beautiful things. These are the artifacts that tell us so much about ancient Egypt. Many of them can be found in the kings' and queens' tombs, such as the great pyramids.

TRACKING TIME

Crops had to be planted at the right time of year, after the great Nile River had flooded. Farmers used a simple measuring rod to tell them when this was going to happen.

Measuring the seasons

The measuring rod was made from a tall **reed**. Notches were cut along the reed. The farmer pushed the reed down into the riverbed. The water rose or fell against the notches. From this, the farmer could tell that the year was divided into three four-month seasons.

Farmers sowed crops, such as papyrus, when the river water was down.

What is it to us?

The measuring rod was like a calendar—it divided the year into seasons. The modern-day calendar came from this early idea.

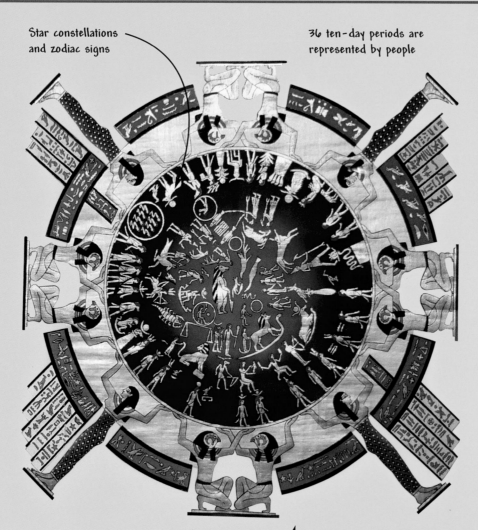

Star constellations and zodiac signs

36 ten-day periods are represented by people

Burying time

Later, ancient Egyptians wanted to measure time more accurately. So they invented a calendar, like the one above. They studied the cycles of the Moon, stars, and Sun to get it right. We divide our year into 12 months. The Egyptians divided theirs into 36 ten-day periods.

Tomb calendars told a dead person's soul what season it was, and if it was day or night. Some of the best calendars have been found painted on tomb walls.

HARVEST HELPERS

The sickle was a tool used by the ancient Egyptians to clear land to grow crops and flowers. Millions of simple sickles helped to produce enough food to sell to other lands. That made Egypt rich. The sickle was also used to cut reeds.

Reeds were used to make:

Mats

Baskets

Paper

What is it to us?

Farming artifacts show us a lot about ancient Egyptian agriculture. The tools they used were very similar to those used in Britain until the 18th century.

Razor-sharp sickles were used to harvest crops.

Tools for toil

Most sickles had long, curved blades made of wood. A groove ran along the length of the blade. This groove was studded with small, razor-sharp **flints**. Many ancient sickles have been found. They were also painted on pots and walls in tombs.

More than one job

Grinding stones **crushed wheat into flour. These useful tools were even placed inside pyramids, so the pharaohs' slaves could use them in the afterlife.**

Laborers worked the land during the farming season. When the fields were flooded, they built great houses, temples, and pyramids. Their tools were also used for more than one task. A hoe dug up soil, but it could also be used to mix up clay to make bricks.

TOOLS OF THE TRADE

The pyramid at Giza is about 475 feet (145 meters) tall. It is amazing how the ancient Egyptians designed such huge pyramids and temples. Their architects and high priests had to draw accurate diagrams. They used a measuring rod to help them.

Rods and lines

Like ancient Egyptian farmers, architects had measuring rods. However, the architects' rods were used to measure height and width of buildings. The rod was a "royal cubit" long. That is about 1.72 feet (0.5 m). Seven lines were carved along its length. Each was a hand-palm's width apart. Tiny measurements were marked in between, to make measuring more accurate.

Most rods were made of wood, with a hinge. The great architect, Kha, was buried with a rod of gold.

Mighty measures

The ancient Egyptians used different measurements for land.

- For small lengths, the "cord measure" was used. It was equal to 100 royal cubits, or 172 feet (52 m).

- For larger lengths, the "river-unit" was used. It was equal to 20,000 royal cubits, or about 6.5 miles (10.5 km).

From rods to arithmetic

Pyramids and temples were huge. The rod was too small to measure such big heights and lengths. So architects had to figure them out. They developed **arithmetic** and **mathematics** using a decimal system, just like we use today.

The pyramids are one of the world's mathematical marvels.

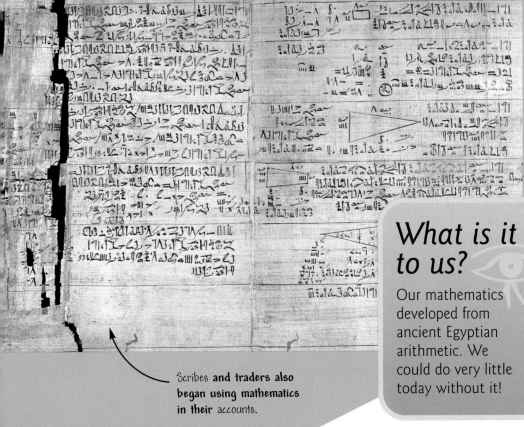

Scribes and traders also began using mathematics in their accounts.

What is it to us?

Our mathematics developed from ancient Egyptian arithmetic. We could do very little today without it!

WEAPON WARFARE

Ancient Egypt's rulers kept sending soldiers to gain more territory from other kingdoms. They also brought back precious items, such as cosmetics, gold, wood, and other treasures. All this wealth made other kingdoms jealous. So Egypt had to defend its borders well. For hundreds of years, their main weapon was the spear.

Weak weapons— enormous armies

Thousands of soldiers with spears sound really scary. The truth is that the spear was weak and slow. That's why armies had to be so enormous. Early spears were wooden poles with sharpened copper heads. By about 2000 BC, bronze heads made spears stronger. There were bronze-headed battle-axes, too.

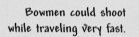
Bowmen could shoot while traveling very fast.

Beaten by technology

In 1700 BC, ancient Egypt learned the hard way that it needed stronger weapons. The Hyksos tribe came thundering into Egypt on chariots. They carried flexible bows that shot arrows far and fast. The Egyptians were forced to develop great chariots and better weapons of their own.

Soldiers were very important to the ancient Egyptians. Hundreds of soldier statues were buried with pharaohs to protect them in the afterlife.

WRITTEN WONDERS

Writing was the best tool for organizing trade, government, religion, and just about everything in ancient Egypt. Hundreds of writers, or scribes, were employed throughout the empire. They wrote mountains of records, lists, and accounts. A scribe's most valuable tool was his writing **palette**.

Writing tools

The writing palette was a bit like a small desk. It was wooden with two deep holes used as inkwells. These held powdered colors called pigments. Pens were laid flat along a carved slender groove.

Being able to read and write were skills to be proud of in ancient Egypt. Some pharaohs had sculptures made that showed them reading or writing.

A scribe's tools

Papyrus paper was expensive to make, so it was used only for very important documents. Scribes first used **hieroglyph** pictures to represent words, then words and sounds. Later they wrote in **hieratic** script, with a symbol for each letter.

Special shapes were drawn around the names of gods, kings, and queens.

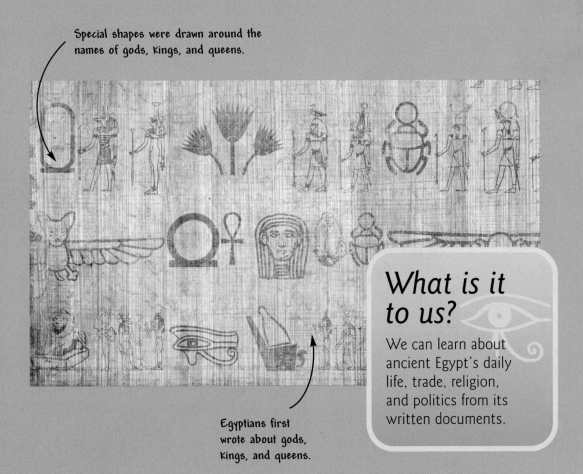

Egyptians first wrote about gods, kings, and queens.

What is it to us?

We can learn about ancient Egypt's daily life, trade, religion, and politics from its written documents.

MAKING MUSIC

Kings and wealthy merchants had a lot of spare time and money to hold magnificent parties and festivals where they listened to music. The oldest and best-loved musical instrument was the harp.

An ancient Egyptian harp

Music in life— and in death

There were many types of harps. Small ones were played so that musicians could dance at the same time. There were also huge harps, which were shown painted on tomb walls. They were the kind played at kings' funerals.

Harps were played at:
- parties
- funerals
- ceremonies

Some harps had only four strings, while others had as many as 22. Egyptians thought that harps were important to their gods. This is why so many kings' tombs had pictures of **harpists**.

Public performance

Kings also showed their power by holding musical processions. In these, soldiers performed powerful fighting dances as the bands played. Bands also performed at great public funeral processions for kings.

The woman on the far right of this picture is playing a reed instrument called a *shawm*. The other women are clapping.

17

BEAUTIFUL BODIES

Almost every man and woman had at least one small blue pottery jar. These jars contained perfumed oils. There were also pots, palettes, grinders, and sticks for all kinds of cosmetics.

Looking good, feeling fine

Ancient Egyptians believed that the mind, body, and spirit were all connected. So it was important to look after the body. Both rich and poor used scented oils and **henna** for their hair. There were even expensive antiwrinkle creams, treatments for baldness, and books on diets.

The ancient Egyptians stored their cosmetics in blue pots like this one.

Eye makeup was put on perfectly. Ancient Egyptians used polished silver, copper, or bronze mirrors to make up their faces.

Eye-catching

Eyes were very important to the ancient Egyptians. They used images of eyes for protection against evil. Dark **kohl** eyeliner made the eyes look larger. They also thought it protected the eyes from infection and insects. Kohl was made from galena—a mineral found around Mount Sinai. Green eyeshadow came from copper **ore**.

What is it to us?

Ancient Egyptians thought beauty was inside them as well as on the surface. Many people still believe that. Henna is still used to color and condition hair, and kohl is still used as eyeliner.

MYSTERIOUS MUMMIES

Mummies found inside tombs show us how the bodies of ancient Egyptians were prepared after death. Their **body tissues** tell us about the kinds of diseases they had. Their stomach contents and teeth show us the foods they ate. What amazing, gruesome treasures these are!

Looking good, feeling... rather dead!

Ancient Egyptians believed strongly in life after death. So they preserved the bodies of the dead in cloths.

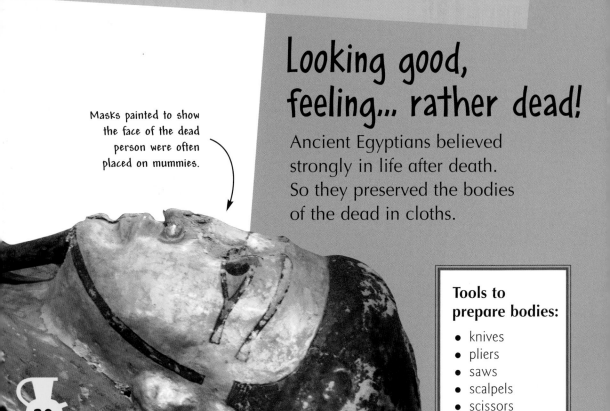

Masks painted to show the face of the dead person were often placed on mummies.

Tools to prepare bodies:

- knives
- pliers
- saws
- scalpels
- scissors

Because the insides of the body rotted, tools were later made to cut out the heart, liver, kidneys, and other organs. A long instrument, like a knitting needle, pulled the brain out through the nostril! All these organs were placed in tall **canopic jars**.

The mummies of kings and queens were placed in painted tombs like this one.

What is it to us?

Many ancient Egyptian surgical instruments are used today to help cure living bodies.

GLOSSARY

accounts Sums that record what has been bought, sold, or made

arithmetic Adding, subtracting, dividing, and multiplying

artifacts Objects that people used a long time ago

body tissues A body's skin, flesh, and organs

canopic jars Tall jars that held body parts. They had stoppers shaped like a human head

flints Very smooth, sharp stones

floodwater Water that rises with a lot of rain or melted snow and covers land

grinding stones Stones used to grind grains or spices into fine powders

harpist A person who plays a harp

henna A leafy plant that makes hair shiny and gives it a red color. It can also be used to paint beautiful patterns, called mendhi, on the hands and feet

hieratic An ancient Egyptian form of writing that used characters rather than pictures

hieroglyph Picture that has a meaning. Hieroglyphs were used in the same way that we use letters to make words

kohl A black powder used to line the eyes

mathematics Using numbers to work things out

ore Metals such as gold or iron that are found in rocks

palette A thin, flat board on which to lay out instruments or dab paints

papyrus A waterside plant and the paper made from the flattened, dried pith inside the plants

pharaoh A king or ruler of ancient Egypt

reed Long, tall thick grass that grows along the riverbank

scribes Writers who are paid to write letters, accounts, and other documents

traders People who buy, sell, or exchange goods